WHEN
YOU ASK ME
WHY

ANNETTE TOWLER

DEDICATION

In memory of Gardner Govan

CONTENTS

ACKNOWLEDGMENTS

Thanks to my poet friends
who have supported me
with their wisdom and encouragement

WHEN YOU ASK ME WHY

When you ask me why, I try to find the words to describe how the closeness of you makes me think of a fireplace, with natural logs burning on a chilly Autumn night as the cat sits beside it, not timid at all as the orange flames jump up and down like a display of musical lights

When you ask me why

When you ask me why, I think of the way you pick up the dishes, insisting that you carry them into the kitchen, to rinse and to place in the dishwasher as I sit on the crumpled, old sofa and stroke the cat's head to relax and to smile when you say what and I reply that I like to look at your face.

When you ask me why, I think of the way that you ask whether I am ticklish, and I reply that I used to be and you respond that I lost the sensation and I respond with a giggle because there is something funny in everything, even when you ask me why.

When you ask me why, it seems infantile to compare you to others of the past because how can I compare the uniqueness of you to the rest, and it is not that you are the best of the best, it is because it is you.

When you ask me why, how can I describe the way that you leave all your guitars lined up in a row on the floor, inviting you to play while I sing along, unaccompanied by a big band or a musical celebrity, just you strumming your guitar remembering what you used to do when you were college age

How can I describe?

When you ask me what, my eyes scan my memory chambers thinking of all the adjectives to use when I look at your face because there is something in your face that makes me quiet, not a sadness that happens when words are left unspoken, but the quietness that comes from a feeling of contentment, a sensation of balm and bliss

What you ask me what, I think of the way you take the gum out of your mouth and place it in the wastepaper basket, wrapped in a piece of tissue and how you kiss me after the disposal, and all I want to say is that I like the taste of you and the gum in your mouth

When you ask me why, I cross out all the usual explanations, your intelligence, your wit, your dark handsome complexion, and I am left with the only explanation that I can find

It is because it is You.

CONVERSATION ABOUT ANOTHER TIME

There is a silence that comes between us after several hours together and it is the kind of silence that only happens when nothing needs to be said

You look into my eyes seeing the joy within me and the conversation starts when I tell you about another time

It was a time when I tell you about the fine cracks in my composure

I learned to stay quiet in the downstairs apartment and the sofa was home

The house was crammed full of an assortment of people, some with and some without a disability that didn't hold them or cramp their style

In the old house between suburbia and the city, a house with basement, first floor, second floor, sky and people ran between all the levels stopping in to see me

When they detected the craquelure on my face, my face as a painting

With the ability to read all the emotions on my face, all the gestures and the flight from the house to the basement

There was no need to say a word

There is no need to say a word

When you tell me that you see the vigor inside of me refreshed after the conflict

RETURN TO EARTH

What happens to us when we die is a conversation that we allude to occasionally when we are alone because the thought of death is something to avoid in chit-chat concerning the weather or the many types of tea that the English drink.

When the topic of what happens to you and I when we leave this world arises, I look up at you and imagine you as a bird flying through the sky, stripped of stress and soaring like a handsome white bird who looks for me, until you find me.

When you find me, I imagine that we merge into each other and become a large white dove that travels around the world looking for places of unrest to heal and to cleanse and inside the bird of peace, we continue to love each other so that the restlessness of the world is softened.

For us, time has no place, we are infinitesimal in our existence because who are we to judge the way in which the planet unfolds again and again as we return to past places that make us sparkle and inside the great white bird we kiss each other again and again, remembering and visiting all the places where we loved for the first time, again and again, soaring around the world, ready and waiting for our inevitable return.

And who are we when we return to the world in human form? Will you still have your facial growth? Will my hair be as fine as silk? These are questions that arise from time to time when I look at you and think about the dreadful possibility that you might die before I do.

Feeling the humanity inside my heart when I look at you and see the fear in you of what might happen if I depart first, and we return to each other without saying a word. Hopeful that we will meet in a heavenly place where I kiss you and you touch my cheek. Our heart crammed full of grace.

NESTLED IN THE HILLS

Shake the snow globe and the flakes crest the sky surrounding the glass
We close our eyes and jump inside
Spinning through the crescent white droplets
Landing on the pavement next to my childhood home
I take you inside the terraced house, little furniture except for the large television set and a chair,
Ensconced in the living room.

Upstairs is my room, complete with single bed where I lay at night
The neighbor listened
To determine if I might cry
I never did
In England, we learn to keep everything proper inside the houses
We soak up the proper manners, taught in all-girl schools.

You and I slip out of the house and run to the top of the street spying
the Old Fort in the distance
I take you there and the drizzle wets our hands
The drips turn to drops and our bodies are encased in water
We run towards the hills
The rain lifts us up with its hands to shield us from the tarmac on
our toes
We skip to the top and read the signs of the Old Fort
Stonehenge of the Iron Age, where I played and skipped as an infant
drawn to the soil and ground of my ancestors.

We blink and the snowdome shakes us into the past again as we run
through downtown Oswald's Tree, the place where I was born and
we are teenagers still ineligible for the first sips of old ale from the
local tavern

We peer into the windows to gaze at the seniors who nurse stout,
bitter, and warm lager on a winter's day in England, giggling at
the absurdity of it all
We arrive through the teleport of snow to a heaven of memories
In a Place that is my home.

FIVE SENSES OF YOU

The scent of you is with me when you are not around
Nostrils sip the air of you
Natural cologne of you
My eyes flick up to the ceiling
Recalling your voice from largo to allegretto
It helps me miss you less
When you are not around
When you are not around, I pretend you are cutting the meat
With your knife and fork, the American way
Cutting the seams of beef with knife
The gentle touch of the silver blade onto the plate
Raise up the fork to bite, touch
I watch your mouth curl and lick the morsels with your tongue
I pretend you are here,
When you are not around

When you are around, the sight of you grabs my heart
Leaving tiny handprints on my skin
Encircling the beats is the touch of you
Your hand in my hand, wrapping your arm around me
Like a scarf for winter, warm and snug inside the quiet space
When you are around
When you disappear for a moment, my mouth waters at the thought
of your kiss
Your mouth wrapped inside my mouth, bodies connecting to our
hearts
The talk of plans and desires, alive in my ears until you come back to
the room

When you are not around, I think of the way you tell me of the verses
inside Genesis and the meaning they have for you, your eyes alive
with fire at the thought that all our senses are intertwined in each
other

The five senses of me and you.

MUSICAL HOUSES

Someone spoke of musical chairs, but I prefer to call it Musical Houses because of the ways in which you show your rituals. The first thought that comes to my mind is the way you drive your oversized vehicle into the garage, while my petite American-built car sits aloft in your parkway. It's the way in which you accommodate me that makes me think of musical houses. The way in which you turn on the radio, guessing that I was a Motown fan back in the day when I also liked The Clash. Together, we hum the words to a Stevie classic, and your hand is on my leg in a magical, musical house wave. The second thought that comes to mind is the way you talk about the mattress, sometimes marshmallow, sometimes too soft and you inquire about my desire to toss the mattress and I say a line from All about Eve. The line about a bumpy ride. The second thought is the way that you laugh. To specify the third way would be to trivialize your character because when I see you curvet from vehicle to doorstep to stair, my heart goes pitter pat. I never cared for Izzat, the Arabic word for reputation, because of the many hats that you wear including the Sherlock and the winter warming one; frankly, I like the way you look at me when I don the your bowler hat that rests in an oversize way on my head. If there was a way I could capture the look on your face when I practice Francais in your presence or the way you say that you love my streams of consciousness, even though I am no Faulkner; I would be a billionaire ten times over. No essence from a bottle of perfume can make me feel the way that you do.

THE PATH DOWN
TO BRADFORD BEACH

Bloated with turkey and stuffing, we meander towards the Upper East Side

I stick by your side even though you encourage me to go ahead

I remind you that my ego is not my amigo to make you smile

I like the way you tilt your head at me as we run along the road

I have taken this road quite often that leads to the four lions and the lighthouse

I have never ventured down the path to Bradford Beach

You point the path to me as we meander down this road we have never

Travelled together before

I realize that it is the first time that I have run with you by your side

You promise to take me there

When we turn around, I say

You have little steps you say

I don't have a big stride I confess

We continue past the lions and discover there are no ghosts to hold us back

A new journey along the road

WHEN YOU ASK ME WHY

The road continues into Lake Park, your favorite spot
We discuss the merits of British gastronomic
We pass the restaurant where you promise to take me sometime
You can wear one of your pretty dresses, you tell me
You point to the steps to take me down to the beach
We can climb the path away from Bradford Beach
It is a route I have never taken
My face lights up with delight when you tell me
That you like my hair long and light
The path is long and inclines enough for me to want to dart to the
top
You watch me dash up the path
I reach the top and pause for a moment so I can see you
The best part of the run is coming backdown to you
We touch for a moment
Our eyes falling towards the beach
Discovering a new route together.

THANKFUL FOR
THE LITTLE THINGS

There is something about the way that the cat wags her tail
Hoping one day that she will return as a dog
It's the little Things

There is something about the way that the cat waits for your descent
Down the stairs, waiting for the pat on the head
It's the little Things

There is something about the way that the cat meows to
Make a formal announcement that issues are resolving
It's the little Things

WHEN YOU ASK ME WHY

When you touch my face in the morning
To let me know you are awake
There is something about your gaze
It's the little Things

You pour the coffee into the China Cup
You watch me sip
And ask me about the different blends of English Tea
It's the little Things

We sit and drink our coffee
With a moment of silence
Before I spurt out my usual stories
Always the little Things

TIK-TOK HANDS

Social media has no time for us
Our hands are laced with lines
Yet somewhere in the space of us
Our youth is quite sublime

I hold your hand to show you
How much you mean to me
Your hands massage my back of bones
Your fingers touch my cheek

We had Tik-Tok hands for ages
Time was linear to us
Yet somewhere in our journey
The world smiled back at us

Tik-Tok says the clock no more
Your hands caress my scars
I run my fingers through your fleeting hair
You touch my wrinkled, youthful heart

Our hands are snug together,
We hold hands to capture time
Because every moment spent with you
Halts the finite climb

THE SNOW IN DOOR COUNTY

There is magic that compels us to walk outside the hotel and feel the
snow
caress our cheeks
You plant two gentle kisses on my forehead
To seal a promise that I made to you

There is a call in the light wind whipping my exposed
neck to remind me of the rawness inside
Until you wrap your arm around me
Muscled from the runs

The softness of the snow slips into our hands
Nails firm with calcium
White mixed with cream along the circular lines
Of our fingers
Your tips that pluck the chords

The vehicle is shrouded in white
We gaze at the thick ribbons of Ivory
Bold in the swipes of nature
Statis in our stance

You open the door and I grab the wiper
My hands ripping through the tresses of snow
Empowered by the beauty of the whiteness
We work as a team, ensuring that the vehicle is clean
A short walk filled with promise for you and I
In a valley of fresh crispness

RHUBARB CRUMBLE

Fresh from a garden in Colorado, gather up the rhubarb
Serve it in a dish in Milwaukee to you
Red around the stems, stewed inside the Dutch pot
The perfume of rhubarb and the crispness of apples steams inside the pot
Chopped into quarters so that the pieces are edible
At the bottom of the bowl
Crested by bread and crumble
All the sweetness you deserve
Flavored with cinnamon to add a touch of spice to your lips
Spoon into the bowl carefully scooping
The French Vanilla ice-cream
Placing a dabble of cream on top of the pudding
To serve to you as you ready yourself
To undo your belt

CAUGHT IN THE PRESENT

It is early morning when we slide out of bed, looking at the temperatures of teens and contemplating whether to leave the slippers on the floor and slide into running shoes.

In a moment of courage, you don your running tights and I don my Wool cap, shivering on the corner of Lake, fidgeting with the watch, waiting for the signal. It is seven o'clock and the residents of Lower East are fast asleep in their beds while we run along the path that leads to the lighthouse.

We catch our breath in the coldness of winter and gaze at the dormant beacon of hope. The lighthouse, surrounded by the stone lions who look at us as if we are ghosts.

Ghosts who have stumbled into a place of silence where there is stillness in the warmth of us. There is warmth between us and I am caught in your presence, as you skip along the path, pointing to the sky that is rich with redness and grey.

If ghosts could speak, what would they tell us of our presence in the world?
We reassure ourselves that we have meaning until we look at each other
Amazed at the absurdity of daily living because how can we enjoy coffee, when the news is black and grey?

Somewhere in the calm, collected presence of the run, our footprints mark the spot of our existence and we want to believe that life is good and every winter we will have the courage to be caught in each other's presence.

MILLION YEARS

We have known each other a million years and the tea still tastes the same
same
A million years since you first called me your sweetheart
A billion eons spinning around the dryer
You carefully fold the sheets and we look into each other's eyes
Each with our own theory of why we are together
For you, something weird and magical happened between us and it is the mindfulness
the mindfulness
That matters
For me, there is the idea of a huge chess game with the kings and queens jockeying for position with fancy dinners and lavish ballrooms
You and I are pawns in the game, carefully moving towards each other and avoiding all the
Trappings of the finest things in life
I like the way you wink
We have known each other a zillion trillion times and every time we speak to each other
It is to share a funny moment, a tender moment
You call it luxurious when my head is close to yours
Discovering that I washed the sheets and you tidied up the cupboards
It is a million galaxies ago when you first held me tight
When you called me sweet pea
A trillion, zillion stars ago
Since the universe clapped its hands.

LOVE IN FAMILIAR PLACES

There is no superhero to come and save us from the screams and
terror of a world filled with power
The love comes in the stillness of the morning when the cat blinks
like a resplendent being, all knowing, all seeing with a wink in the eye
Like an oracle, the cat gazes out of the window, beckoning us to come
study the birds, the sparrows whose plain coat warms us to the beauty
of those who live on the margins
The marginalized call to us in unfamiliar places – the beach, the alley
by the side of the house – asking us to listen, just listen
In the quiet of the morning, we speak to each other through touch
and glances that tell us of a universe where every animal receives a pat
on the head or a treat in the dish
We close our eyes and wrap a bandage around the bird that hobbles
or the cat with one eye, wishing we could do the same for all the
creatures on this imperfect planet
Loving each other as the hoot of the owl silences us
with the magnitude of all the glories hidden in our petite and
promising garden

CHICKEN DINNER IN JUNE

For decades the men of Shorewood invite residents from around the city to collect and taste the roasted chicken, crisp with skin so succulent it is a sin to rip it off in pursuit of a leaner body

The sign for the chicken dinner hides in the garage next to the single, red car and we spy it every time that we enter the garage to remove our hybrid bikes

You have the lean, giddy up and gallop bike and I have the stout, feminist bike to plod slowly from house to coffee shops

One day we overexert ourselves on the bikes in a warm day of June and we look at the sign again and appreciate that it is the night to celebrate poultry and we dash up the road, endorphins still high from the ride on the trail, and we wait in line, smelling the poultry, a yearning for barbecue etched in our bones

Back at the house that feels like a ranch, we open the boxes and we snort and sniff, craving the meat and we pull out the knives and forks from the drawer, lift the condiments from the refrigerator, and rip the lids off the coleslaw

Seated at the table, we smile at each other and our eyes gaze at the chicken feast, content to be together in this land of beasts and wheat.

YOGA AT THE TOP

The house climbs up to three levels
With a staircase spiraling up to the attic, elegant twister leading us
and beckoning us to the mats on the floor
We elongate and stretch our arms up in to the air
I call out and you repeat
Warrior One because you are a warrior and I stretch back
to being Peaceful as we contemplate the nature of love and how to
demonstrate it in our daily life
Is it when you bend your knee and whisper
Warrior Two?
Or is it when I smile and utter namaste?
Breath into our nostrils
Breath out from our lungs
Glistening ageing bodies from the bends and traps of living
Finding trust in each other as we focus on the moment, the warrior
now, present in time
Because we want to keep repeating this
Wanting time to never run out

UNFINISHED

Physically you have gone and you are still here in my soul
The soul that rises up in the morning and touches the photograph
Next to the bed, which we bought from the overzealous salesman
Who managed to close and get the coffee

In spite of your sudden departure, I still speak to you through
Consonants, adjectives, superlatives, and sighs
I feel you every time I lace up my running shoes
That you picked out for me in the sale of last year's model
A reminder that we are both thrifty because our childhood demanded it
Sometimes I wonder if you hear me speak to you aloud even though you aren't here
I know it's perfectly acceptable to speak to you
The only problem is if I reply to myself
Is it randomness that brought us together or a perfectly designed puzzle, dreamed up
By an imperfect deity?

WHEN YOU ASK ME WHY

Does it have to be finished this connection of ours?
Should I be like Bette Davis in Now Voyager
Merely asking for the stars?

I cry out to other widows, some were married, some were not
Trying to find my new identity in a language that is foreign
To my ears and to my voice
I'm not allowed to say widowed but it's acceptable to say bereaved

At other times, I pretend that I am gone instead of you and I imagine
I am a ghost
Who hides in the attic, only descending when you are sad
I hold you in my arms and say I love you in the night
I imagine that you hear my words and for you it is a moment of
delight

Reality sinks in when I sort through all your clothes, laying them out
into
Neat piles of donations and socks with holes
It is in that moment that the sadness envelops me
I feel you lift me up to the top of the stairs
Reminding me to be free.

ONE OF THOSE WEEKS

Do you remember how we got all the grading done and they gave us a new yard?

They installed down spouts and new gutters into our craftsman house and the place was transformed

Well, I can tell you, it's been quite the week because I needed to do laundry and I walked into the basement to find puddles of water, spread out neatly on the floor

In a moment of impulsiveness, I phoned several basement men and they provided quotes

One flashy salesman wanted half a year's salary and provided a presentation on the importance of drains and the formidable sump pump

I hired the other reasonable basement man who asked me if I believe in Jesus

And of course, in the same week, another incident

Can you believe it?

Someone drove into my car when it was parked in the lot leaving a dent on the passenger side but I can still drive the car to get to the hospital

So I can see you in the final moment, gasping the last breath

FINISHED BUSINESS

Led Zeppelin is playing as you climb up onto the first ledge
A gobble of snow like your first shave with butter
On the second step you almost lose your balance
Wanting to step in reverse to the familiar bathroom
Full of razor blades, a soft Egyptian robe, and the tub
Ruined by inadequate plumbing
The third step is easy like a hop into the walk-in shower
Not one of your preferences
You wait for the next, not caring about the number of steps to climb
Because all the while a tune is playing and it sounds like Thin Lizzy
Having another tumbler of whisky and you wonder if you will meet
Irish Phil
at the very top of the staircase
You know where you are going
The shower door opens and, you step into a winter wonderland
Of Bird baths, feeders, chipmunks, and rabbits
The dove flies into your hands, and you gaze down at me
Looking outside at the snow
And release the bird into the air
It lands on the top of the feeder, softly humming the song of all birds.

ABOUT THE AUTHOR

I was born in England and moved to the United States in the early 1990s. I enjoy my job as a therapist and in my spare time I like to run. I live in an old house in Milwaukee and have a sweet cat called Marsha.